Vicki Lansky

WELCOMING YOUR SECOND BABY

Revised and Updated

the book peddlers

deephaven, mn

Special thanks to Editors: Kathryn Ring, Toni Burbank,
                          Sandra L. Whelan and Julie Surma
Cover Design: Nancy MacLean
Illustrator: Jack Lindstrom

The contents of this book have been reviewed for accuracy and appropriateness by Jan
Goodwalt, R.N., of the St. Paul Hospital, and Joan Reivich of Philadelphia's Booth
Maternity Center. Material for children at a birth has been reviewed and enhanced by
Penny Simkin and Jeanine Bontrager.

Thanks also to Dr. Burton White for his comments.

**Special thanks to the parents who shared their words and feelings. Their quotes are
reprinted with permission from Vicki Lansky's** *Practical Parenting*™ **newsletter.**

We appreciate the right to reprint:
"Some Things Don't Make Any Sense at All," by Judith Viorst.
Reprinted with the permission of Atheneum Publishers
from <u>*If I Were in Charge of the World and Other Worries,*</u>
copyright © 1981 by Judith Viorst.

THE NEW BABY AT YOUR HOUSE/Cole
  Photo: copyright © 1985 by Hella Hammid
HOW YOU WERE BORN/Cole
  Photo: copyright © Wolf Heinrichs/The Image Bank

WELCOMING YOUR SECOND BABY
A Bantam Book / August 1984
Bantam Revised Edition / March 1987
The Book Peddlers Revised Edition / September 1990

ISBN 0-916773-12-4

For group sales or quantity discounts contact:
The Book Peddlers
18326 Minnetonka Boulevard
Deephaven, MN 55391
(612) 475-3527

0 9 8 7 6 5 4 3 2 1

Contents

Introduction

A Welcome Addition

The thought of having a second child is often overwhelming to parents. The first has already taken so much of your love, time, and attention, so much of the space in your home, so much of your income, that you wonder how you'll possibly manage. And you wonder, perhaps, if you'll ever be able to love a second child as much as you do the first. Will there be enough love for both? Are you being disloyal to your firstborn by forcing a sibling on him or her? Will your second child be an intruder in your family, a competitor for your attention and love? In short, will your second child be a welcome addition?

Ideally, a sibling will bring your firstborn down to earth a bit, teach him or her to share, and provide a live-in playmate in childhood and lifelong love and companionship. Together, you'll all be a real family.

Two things you can plan on for sure are that your second child will not be a replica of the first, even though they may look alike, and that you can't predict, totally, the reception of the second by the first. Whatever the age of the first, whatever the spacing between the two, the firstborn may hate or adore the baby; may regress to babyhood or grow up in amazing ways; may be indifferent to or fascinated by the baby. Of course some part of the older child's reception of the baby will depend upon his or her age, on how dependent he or she has been on you, and on his or her emotional maturity, but some aspects of the reception are simply unexplainable, a matter of personality and the circumstances of the moment.

I've included here many, many ideas to help you help your child adjust to the arrival of the new baby. You'll find lots of good ideas here but please, don't feel you need to try them all! There is such a thing as too much of a good thing. You *can* over-prepare your child by too much attention to preparation.

By the way, don't forget to have yourself prepared—for child birth, that is. Take that refresher course you don't think you have time for. It will really help. Trust me, you really don't remember it all. Plus, it's good quality time for you and your partner.

Relax. Enjoy your child. Enjoy your pregnancy. The best (and the most tiring) is yet to come!

Vicki Lansky

SOME THINGS DON'T MAKE ANY SENSE AT ALL

by Judith Viorst

My mom says I'm her sugarplum,
My mom says I'm her lamb.

My mom says I'm completely perfect
Just the way I am.

My mom says I'm a super-special
wonderful terrific little guy.

My mom just had another baby.

Why?

1

How Can I Best Prepare My Child for the Birth of a New Baby?

Your first step, obviously, is to announce that the baby's on the way. The "whens" and "hows" of this depend not only on the age of your first child, but also on that child's interest in the event and relative maturity. Each child will handle the news differently, in his or her own unique way, no matter how you prepare your child. And the child who is initially pleased about becoming a big sister or brother may have a change of heart once the baby is born, or even six months later.

No matter what your child's age, don't be surprised, if after you share the big news, your child just drops the subject for awhile.

When you tell the child will depend on the child's age to a large extent. A pregnancy that seems long enough to you will be a lifetime to a child whose concept of time is still fuzzy.

We worry not only about our child's acceptance of the new baby, but also about our own. ("Will I ever be able to love this child as much as my first one?") We fall in love with each child in a different way and at a different pace. Don't worry. It does happen in the natural sequence of things.

When to Share Your Great News With Your Child

• Ideally, tell a preschooler about two or three months before the birth, but realistically, you'll share the news when you've made it public. You may be pushed into telling an observant child who notices that Mom is getting "fat."

• Don't tell any child until you're ready for the whole world to know. A child can't be expected to keep such a secret.

• But don't tell a child too soon, in case you miscarry. The child might feel guilty and in some way responsible for the loss of the baby. If you decide to tell the child right away, be sure to offer full and honest explanations if problems arise later.

• Don't wait too long to tell any child. He or she may overhear you talking about your pregnancy, or a friend or neighbor may let the word slip. Your child could become unduly worried because you're always tired or because you're occasionally sick without explanation. The boredom of waiting a long time for the baby to come is not as bad for the child as is the feeling that something strange and secret is going on.

• When explaining to a young child when the baby is due, tie the birth to an event instead of to a month or week— "after Christmas," "during your spring vacation from nursery school"—but don't pinpoint it *too* exactly.

Sharing Age-Appropriate Reproductive Information

• Show your readiness to answer questions about birth and reproduction by your tone of voice and your patience. Give assurance that it's all right to ask *any* question.

• Use the correct words for the parts and functions of the body in your discussions. They're no harder to learn than other words, and they won't have to be unlearned later. (Use the word *uterus*, not *stomach*, for instance.)

• Get suitable books about babies and birth very early in your pregnancy, perhaps even before you break the news to your child. Read them together and make them available for casual perusal by the child (see reviews at the end of this chapter).

• Don't be surprised if your child of 2 or so has no questions, or very few, about the baby. A statement like, "Mothers have a special place where the baby grows until it's ready to be born" may be all that's required in the way of explaining reproduction.

• Do be prepared to repeat whatever facts you do give *often*.

• Explain the stretch of a mother's vagina by putting a tennis ball in a tube sock to show how the opening easily stretches and resumes its narrow opening.

• Expect lots of questions from your preschooler. He or she will probably want details about "what's going on inside there": how the baby eats, sleeps, goes to the bathroom, and other such practical information. Try not to answer more than what's asked.

• On the other hand, don't be alarmed if your preschooler doesn't ask any questions. For some children, the baby doesn't seem real until it actually appears. Some children need the physical presence of the baby before they become interested and start asking questions.

• But if you have the feeling that your child is taking an "if-I-ignore-it-it-will-go-away" attitude, you may want to introduce the subject yourself, so he or she will realize that the baby is real and will be arriving.

> We showed our child pictures of intrauterine development, and took him to childbirth films. He saw a sex education special on PBS. If we had it to do over, we would *not* prepare him so well. We put too much emphasis on the new baby, and he reacted.
> *Dana Clark, Santa Barbara, CA*

Preparing Your Child for Life With a New Baby

• Don't tell a child of any age how he or she is going to feel about the baby. "You're going to love the baby," and "You're going to have such fun playing with the baby and helping me care for the baby" may express your heart's desires, but they may only serve to irritate your child or set him or her up for conflict if your child doesn't feel the way you predicted.

• Stress the positive and give your child status by saying things like, "You're going to be a big brother," rather than, "You're going to have a baby brother or sister."

• Stress the fact, especially to a young child, that the gender of the unborn baby will be a "surprise." (Of course, if you have amniocentesis or a sonagram and know, that's a different matter.)

• Take advantage of the unknown sex of the baby to encourage nonsexist thinking by pointing out that "Girls can _____ too," and "Boys can _____ too." (You may see a bit of jealousy already developing if your child wants the baby to be of the opposite sex from himself or herself.)

• Let your child fantasize about the baby by drawing pictures of how he or she thinks it will look. The drawings may offer you an opportunity to correct misconceptions or provide explanations.

• "Borrow" a baby, or baby-sit one regularly, with two thoughts in mind. First, your child will see how infants act and how much care they need, and second, you'll have a chance to practice having more than one to care for. (And perhaps the other mother will owe you some baby-sitting time when your second baby is born.)

• Better yet, expose your child to more than one infant. Young ones, especially, sometimes have trouble imagining a sibling similar to but not identical to a baby they've seen.

• Let your child see a nursing mother, if possible, so that if you breast-feed, it won't seem shocking or strange.

• Don't let the child think the baby will be a playmate; be clear about the fact that babies do little but eat, sleep, and cry.

• Begin to share child care between spouses, if you don't already, so your child won't expect Mother's care exclusively.

• Point out pictures of newborns in magazines to prepare your child for the way a newborn looks. Explain that babies have no teeth, and that there will be a scab where the umbilical cord was.

• Also point out older babies, to let your child know that babies do change as they get older.

• Remember that rational explanations about an impending future event are basically useless for a child under the age of 2.

When our last child was on the way, our girls were 7 and 8. I bought two very good books with lots of pictures explaining the hows and whys of birth. They loved seeing how "their" baby was developing. They were as excited as my husband and I were. It's been three years now, and the poor "baby" has had three mothers–he can't get away with much!

Susan Lipke, Harietta, MI

Baby Books

There are many wonderful books like the two mentioned here that show pictures of babies which an older child can enjoy now and your new baby will enjoy later.

Babies
by Gyo Fujikawa
Grosset & Dunlap, 1963

A board book with bright, attractive drawings showing multi-ethnic babies that is a classic.

The Baby's Book of Babies
by Sabrina Withall
Harper & Row, 1983

A book of black and white photographs of babies' faces— up close and personal!

Promoting Self-esteem for the New Big Brother or Sister

• Check with your hospital, doctor, or childbirth instructor to see if sibling classes are offered in your area for children whose parents are expecting. Such classes, appropriately geared to children's ages, can be very helpful.

• Make big changes, such as moving the child to a big bed, completing toilet training, or giving up the bottle, well before the baby's expected birth, so the child will feel that he or she is growing up, not being pushed out (see regression, page 72).

• Let your child come with you to check-ups and have the doctor answer any questions your child may have. Doctors often share the ultrasound images with the soon-to-be sibling.

• Don't deprive your toddler of your attention, but don't go overboard in the other direction, either. Go out reasonably often (with a reliable sitter in charge, of course) and insist on some quiet time for yourself, all to help prepare your child for the new demands there will be on your time.

• If you don't send your child to preschool or a play group, don't be afraid to start your own to get your child used to being around other kids.

• Get out your photo albums and look together at pictures of your child as an infant.

• Don't pile on too many gifts and treats before the birth, or after it either, or you'll be sending a guilt-laden message to your child.

> Our 2 1/2-year-old always knew we were getting ready to leave him when we gathered up the pillows for our childbirth classes. He'd immediately throw a full-scale tantrum, going so far as to hold his breath and pass out. We'd go anyway, knowing from hard experience that he'd come to and be all right with the sitter. But I must admit that leaving the house with our child purple and unconscious on the floor pretty much took the fun out of it.
>
> *Ellen S., Minneapolis, MN*

> My 5-year-old daughter would talk to the baby putting her mouth close to my belly button. (Since the baby was inside me I could hear what replies he was thinking and tell her.) The baby would get furious if someone was mean to her, and would take her side.
>
> *C. Calzada, Miami, FL*

Other Ways to Help Prepare Your Child for the Baby's Birth

• Speak of the baby as *ours*, not as yours or the child's.

• Get a baby doll for your toddler if he or she doesn't have one, or outfit an old one with new clothes and some new equipment. Be sure the doll is immersible; it will undergo some bathing later.

• Unpack your child's old baby clothes together and recall stories about his or her infancy while you do.

• Shop for a new baby outfit together.

• Consider, if you take down the crib, not just moving it to another room but storing it away for a while. A child's bed is very personal. You might even want to paint it a different color so it won't stir up memories . . . and resentments. Or trade crib or stroller items with a friend so it doesn't seem like the new baby is "taking things."

• Make use of your family pet to help your child learn gentleness in playing with it. Stress its value as a friend and companion—it may have to sit in for you occasionally!

• Let your preschooler in on your discussion of the baby's name and other plans and decisions. Listen to his or her ideas and talk about them too. But don't make promises about selecting his or her choice of the baby's name. You might consider using it as a nickname.

• Let your child talk to the baby using the navel as a microphone.

• Let your preschooler feel the baby kicking and listen to the heartbeat with a stethoscope. Some toy stethoscopes work surprisingly well.

• Invite your child to do stretching and muscle-strengthening exercises with you. Leg raises and pelvic rocks are usually especially appealing.

Preparing a 1-Year-Old Child for a New Baby

Sorry to mislead you but there really is nothing you can DO to prepare your young "older" sibling for the baby's arrival. Yes, let your child participate in new baby preparations, but don't assume it will be meaningful.

Having two children under two years of age will press you with physical as well as emotional demands.

Rather than trying to make your first child grow up faster, you'll probably do better for everyone if you just lower your expectations and let your toddler be "babyish" too. Rather than trying to prepare your child for the baby or explain the birthing process, try to spend extra time *now* with your older baby.

When the new baby arrives:

• Get household and/or new baby help so you can spend some one-on-one time with your older "baby" daily, or at least weekly. It's your best investment in your family life. Help can be hired or enlisted.

• Make time for yourself, even if it's only 1/2 hour of privacy or a nap. If you fall apart, you're no good to either baby.

Does Spacing Affect Adjustment?

We feel the most important help our older child had was a good three years of our attention before she had a sibling. This got her off to a good start and almost eliminated any rivalry problems we might have had.

Candace Waldrum, Paris, TX

Our son Matt was 19 months old when we brought his new brother, Patrick, home. His first hello was to jump into the baby's crib while it was occupied. Things got steadily worse until big brother made the adjustment of sharing Mom and Dad. Somehow Patrick has managed to survive a year and eight months, and a change has gradually taken place. The little kid who used to just lie there is suddenly lots of fun.

Mary Ann Koenigsfeld, Charles City, IA

Our children are four and one-half years apart. Our oldest had a "full turn" at being a baby and fully welcomed his sister. Now, at 10 1/2 and 6, they seem to be secure in their own persons.

Betsy Durham, Waterford, CT

My brother and I were 18 months apart and great buddies, but I still remember the desire for more individual attention. My children are eight years apart, and both have benefited from individual attention—but are not buddies at all. I doubt there is an ideal spacing.

Beverly Audeh, Huntsville, AL

Preparing Yourself for Some Changes in Lifestyle

• Be aware that in most cases, until the last part of pregnancy, a mother can pick up a toddler, unless the doctor advises otherwise. Lifting may affect your back, but not your in-utero baby.

• If you can't pick the child up, provide a little stool for getting into and out of the high chair and crib or bed. Hug your toddler often when you're siting down or playing on the floor.

• Expect a tantrum or crying jag when you leave to go out alone if you haven't done it a great deal, especially if the child knows you're going to your childbirth class or somewhere else related to the baby.

Preparing Your Older Child or Teenager for the New Baby

• Look upon your pregnancy as an excellent opportunity to read about and discuss human sexuality, reproduction, and family life with your preteen or teenager.

• Don't insist that your youngster read straight through every book you supply; leave books and magazine articles in a convenient place for casual scanning.

• To help your children understand how difficult it is for you to pick up things left on the floor, strap a large stuffed animal or pillow around their waist, and then ask them to help you pick up toys.

• Don't make your older child dread the baby's birth by talking a great deal about how much help he or she is going to be.

• Give a special "baby notebook" to a child who would enjoy keeping a journal and designate him or her as the "Baby Reporter."

• Together, write a list of people and phone numbers who that child can be responsible for calling when the baby is born.

• Prepare yourself to deal with the fact that your teenager may be embarrassed about the fact that you are pregnant and that there will be an infant in the family. Discuss other families you know who have "late" babies and point out the fun they have.

Preparing Your Pet for a New Baby

If you've acquired a pet after the arrival of your first child, you'll find your pet will have accommodations to make to a new baby in the house.

• Allow your pet to explore and investigate baby items and furnishings before the baby arrives (though don't let a cat get used to sleeping in the baby's crib). You might even bring home a baby blanket you've used in the hospital before baby comes home to introduce your baby's "scent" to your pet.

• Be sure your dog is free of fleas. A trip to the groomer while you're at the hospital might be helpful.

"Birds & Bees" Books to Read to Your Child

Your pregnancy is the perfect time to share reproductive information and read-together books are the easiest place to start. With any books, the most important message is the one conveyed by your reading of it. No book has to be read in its entirety, and children will express interest in different information at different ages. Take time to ask and answer questions that arise as you read. At first you may be uncomfortable answering some questions correctly, but it's worth doing. As adults, we often don't use the correct reproductive terms, but the more we use these words, the more comfortable we become with them and the more comfortable our children become too. Don't let old embarrassments get in the way.

Being Born
by Kitzinger & Nilsson
Grosset & Dunlap, 1986

This beautiful edition of in-utero photographs and the birth experience is worth searching out. Many of Nilsson's photos can be found in his classic book, *A Child Is Born*, often more widely available in bookstores. This edition of *Being Born* is more appropriate to share with young children, and equally beautiful.

How Babies Are Made
by Andry & Schepp
Little, Brown & Co., 1969/1979

Photographs of colored paper sculpture to illustrate the story of reproduction make this 84-page book unique. It's both abstract and realistic. The text is simple, emphasizing a somewhat old-fashioned "birds and bees" approach in the beginning, but finishing up with enough specifics to satisfy most.

How You Were Born
by Joanna Cole
William Morrow & Co., 1984

A simple text explains prenatal development from conception to birth. The drawings explain cell division and growth in-utero at 3, 6 and 9 months as well as the birth process. After-birth black-and-white photographs of different families illustrate new baby behavior and family joy.

"Where Did I Come From?"
by Peter Mayle
Lyle Stuart, Inc., 1973

This large-format book calls itself "the facts of life without any nonsense." Its approach is humorous and frank, its colored illustrations cartoon-like. The aim is to have fun with the subject, and it covers lovemaking, orgasm, conception, and growth inside the womb using the same humorous approach.

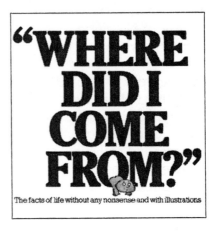

Making Babies
by Sarah B. Stein
Walker & Co., 1974

This square-format book with black-and-white photographs offers a simple yet honest text. Sexual differences are explained in both animals and children. The book lacks reproductive information and is really geared toward the very young child. The text offers side-by-side copy for the adult and the child.

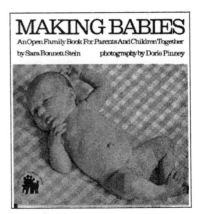

So That's How I Was Born!
by Robert Brooks, M.D.
Simon & Schuster, 1983

Susan Perl's delightful, colored illustrations follow Joey as he learns about how he was born. The story is simple and direct, emphasizing the process of growth within mother and his birth. It covers family feelings and even belly buttons! This is the perfect book for those who want to get information across without being too preachy about it.

See How You Grow
by Patricia Pearse &
  Edwina Riddell
Barron's, 1989

A "lift-the-flap" book that tastefully introduces children to the concept of a baby growing inside their mom. Shows the developing baby at 3, 6 and 9 months. Gently answers developmental questions.

Where Do Babies Come From?
by Margaret Sheffield
Alfred A. Knopf, 1979

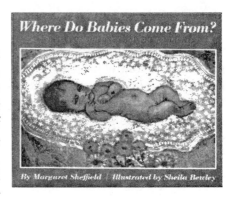

This is a 33-page hardcover book on colored paper with sensitive, anatomically-specific full-page pastel paintings. It is explicit without being stark. The brief accompanying text explains the process of conception and birth. It also does an especially good job of explaining differences between the sexes, describing the parts of the body in correct terms.

Mama, Daddy, Baby and Me
by Lisa Gewing, Spirit Press, 1989. 1499 Masonic Ave. San Francisco, CA 94117

While there is virtually no reproductive information in this book, it is good for the very young child with whom you wish to introduce the idea of a baby's arrival without specific reproductive information. Simple language and soft, realistic illustrations.

2

How Can I Help My Child Adjust to My Absence While I'm in the Hospital?

The younger your child is, and the less often he or she has been left with sitters in your absence, the more upsetting your stay in the hospital will be and the longer it will seem to the child whose time perception isn't well developed. One 8 year-old, when asked how long his mother was in the hospital to have her baby, responded "a month." In fact, she was there only four days!

Some parents try to go out a little more often during the pregnancy and some take a short "for-parents-only" trip or two as a sort of rehearsal. The main preparation for a young child is to make sure he or she knows exactly what will happen while Mom's in the hospital—where he or she will be eating and sleeping and who will be in charge—and that the hospital stay won't be very long. Other preparations can be as elaborate as you wish or can take time to make. Taking your child to a hospital-sponsored sibling-to-be class is a good way to introduce him or her to the hospital and the people who work there. It may also help convince him or her that the hospital is a good place with good people, not a place to be dreaded or feared.

Check with your hospital as early as possible about their policy on having children visit the maternity ward. Most hospitals do allow this now, unless there are special circumstances. If children aren't allowed, you can perhaps plan to visit with your child in the lobby or lounge. Or discuss the possibility of early discharge with your doctor—but only if you'll have good help at home.

Preparing Your Child for Your Hospital Stay

• Try to take your child with you for one or more of your regular checkups, perhaps to hear the heartbeat, but at least to meet the doctor and see the place you visit so often.

• Take the child to the hospital you'll be going to. Have lunch and visit the gift shop. If you can, visit the maternity ward and let the child peek into a room, to see how you'll be living while you're there. Point out a phone in a room or in the hall, and say that's where you'll be calling from when you call home. Discuss what his or her visit to you in the hospital will be like.

• Explain very carefully to the child what will happen to him or her while you're in the hospital—where he or she will be staying, and who will care for him or her. The best plan is to keep your child at home with Dad, a relative, or a familiar baby-sitter. The more normal things are, the less difficult it will be for your child.

• Also explain your alternative plan for the day or night you leave for the hospital, if there's any possibility you'll have to make changes (if a sitter can't be reached, for example).

• Tell your child about the possibility that mommy may go to the hospital while he or she is asleep or at school, as well as who will be there to be with your child if this should occur.

Before You Go to the Hospital

• Tape some bedtime stories for a young child, to be played while you're gone. And don't forget to say good night at the end of each.

• Put a picture of yourself in the child's room. And have your child pick out a photo of him or herself for you to take to the hospital so the new baby can "see" his or her older sibling.

• Ask your child to take care of something for you while you're gone—your favorite scarf, a piece of jewelry or pottery—and search together for the best place in his or her room to keep it.

• Tell your child you'll be calling every day from the hospital. If he or she is old enough to use the phone, write down the number.

• Make a few practice calls when you're away from home, if your child isn't used to your telephone voice.

• Hide a few small gifts around the house. When you call from the hospital, you'll be able to tell your child where to look for them.

• Make or buy a little "welcome" present (such as a bib) for the sibling to give to the new baby when you come home.

• Give your child plenty of opportunity to get used to whoever will care for him or her while you're gone. If the child will be staying with Grandma or another relative or friend, set up an overnight visit, so the house and bedroom will be familiar.

I was at home during most of my labor and this upset my two boys—perhaps better to go to the hospital sooner. They visited me the next day in the hospital and found it hard to understand why I couldn't come home right away!
Mrs. H. Skinner, N. Vancouver, B.C.

Shortly Before the Baby Is Due

• Let your child help you pack your hospital bag and think of things to put in. Remember stamps and notepaper, reading material for both parents, and coins for phone calls.

• Be sure to tell your child that, yes, you are going to the hospital, but you are also coming back.

• Take along a photo of your child and let him or her know it will be placed where you can easily see it.

• Prepare postcards or notes to mail your child from the hospital.

• Get the child to make you some drawings to help decorate the hospital room.

• While you're gone and for your convenience when you get home, keep up with the laundry; stock your cupboards with staples; and freeze casseroles, breads, and desserts for future use.

• Write thank-you notes as you receive gifts for the baby, so you won't have them all to do at once when you're busiest.

• Have a "practice day," with Mom resting in her room and the rest of the family fending for itself. (More power to you if you can pull this one off!)

• Make a "birthday" cake with your older child and freeze it. When you and the new baby arrive home, defrost the cake and have a small party for the baby.

When You're in the Hospital

• Make frequent calls to your child. They needn't be lengthy. Talk about the baby, but not exclusively, and don't forget the most important message: "I love you, and I'll be home soon."

• Buy or borrow an instant camera and send home to your child a photo of the baby, one of you with the baby, and another of you alone.

• Ask your child to water or help water certain plants.

• Tape the sound of the baby crying and send the tape home for your child.

When Your Child Visits You at the Hospital

• Don't build up the child's visit to the hospital because if he or she has a cold, a visit would not be possible.

• Don't allow other guests when your child visits you. Let the first visit, at least, be for family only.

• Remember your child is anxious to see you—not the baby.

• Greet your child *without* your new infant in your arms.

• Have a gift at the hospital from the baby for the older child.

• Let the nurse present a baby doll (bought by you) to your child, so he or she can have a "baby" from the hospital too.

• Pick out a small soft toy as a gift for the new baby from the older sibling that you take to the hospital and can keep in the baby's nursery crib. It will also help them "recognize" their new baby brother or sister when they look in the nursery.

• Take photographs of the children together.

• See if the nurse will tape a photo of the big sister or brother on the baby's crib to make the baby easier to locate when looking in the nursery window.

• Plan your child's hospital visit at the time of day when he or she is not hungry or tired.

• Have the person who brought your child for the visit take him or her home, especially if it's Daddy, to avoid another separation.

• Let the child hold the baby. Don't be surprised if the older child's attention span is brief and there is more interest in your hospital bed's mobility than the new baby.

• Be prepared for your young child to cry when it's time to leave, or to show anger at you for being away from home. A crying jag or a venting of strong feelings is understandable in light of what to him or her seems a very long separation from you. Don't be embarrassed, the staff is used to this behavior.

Coming Home

• If the child is home when you arrive from the hospital, try to have someone else carry the baby into the house. Pay special attention to your older child for at least a few minutes.

• Put a 24-hour moratorium on visitors. This is another day for family only.

• Let your child come with Daddy to pick you up at the hospital, if possible.

• Spend the first day home with everyone in bed for the day

• Or arrange for the child to visit someone and be brought home after you and the baby are settled. If you do this, devote your full attention to the child for as long as possible when he or she comes home.

• Be prepared for your child to express conflicting emotions in response to the baby. He or she may be surprised (despite your warnings) that the baby cries so much and doesn't seem to understand anything.

• Plan to indulge yourself, if at all possible, with cleaning help, an occasional baby-sitter to play with your older child, or a whole day in bed when Daddy's home. Don't fall into the trap of believing that you're indispensable and that nothing will be done right unless you do it. Relax and accept help gratefully when it's offered.

• If Dad can take paternity leave, it should start now!

Some children have been known to be happy, angry, sad or to even disregard mom's and/or baby's arrival home from the hospital. Don't be hurt if you experience a reception of little interest or downright indifference. It's often a mask for feelings of abandonment.

My son, then 2 1/2, didn't really understand what was about to happen even though it was carefully explained. On the way out of the hospital he was in my lap in the wheelchair and the new baby was held by the nurse—not Mommy or Daddy.

Jerri Oyama, Northbridge, CA

My husband had our cassette tape recorder on, and we now have on tape my 3-year-old's response to meeting his younger brother. It's priceless.

Diane Phillips, Milwaukee, WI

Gender Baby Blues

For most parents, having expectations as to the sex of one's unborn child is just a natural part of pregnancy. Parents who already have one child or more of one sex understandably experience feelings that are stronger in expectation of a specific sex than first time parents. Yet parents are often unprepared for having a child of the opposite sex from what they had hoped for. It's normal to feel disappointment, failure, resentment and a feeling of guilt for all of these just stated feelings. If this is your reaction, realize that you're not alone. But it is important to resolve these feelings as quickly as possible—or get help with overcoming them, so as not to affect your relationship with your newborn baby.

Children, too, often have gender preferences. A child asking for a same sex sibling is in all likelihood just asking for a playmate. A child asking for an opposite sex sibling may fear competition, believing an opposite sex sibling will pose less of a threat. But even then, that might not be the case. Sometimes a preference is verbalized by a child from something as minor as a statement overheard from another child.

Reassure your child that no matter what the sex of the new baby, he or she won't be replaced by this new family member. Also verbalize that boys and girls are all able to do the same things.

3

What If We Want
Our Child to Be
Present at the
Birth of the Baby?

Parents who expect normal, uncomplicated births sometimes wish to share the experience with their children. Your child's age and emotional development will weigh heavily in your decision about whether or not to have him or her present at the birth. When you've made up your mind, ask your child. Even very young ones may have a definite preference. Be sure to make it clear that the child can change his or her mind at any time.

Some parents do not believe children should be present at a birth; they feel the experience is too traumatic. Many discourage allowing children under 4, especially, to participate. They say the mother may be so concerned about the child that she won't be able to concentrate properly on the birth process and will instead try to put on a performance for the child.

In the March 1987 Journal of the American Academy of Child

and Adolescent Psychiatry, a study reported that siblings in the delivery room may feel more anxiety than is recognized by their parents. To the parents' surprise most of the youngsters felt anxious about seeing the birth. Children under the age of five often didn't know what to expect despite coaching. Often it was more a case of the child wishing to be near mom rather than at the birth.

On the pro side of the controversy, other parents feel that the experience will not be frightening to a child if it's handled properly. They believe participation in a birth gives a child a deep appreciation of childbirth and of life itself, and promotes the feeling of family. Some have even advanced the belief that sibling rivalry will be reduced and the sibling bond will be stronger because of the child's presence in the birthing room.

In a study of fifty-five home births in Salt Lake City almost one-third of the women felt that sibling rivalry was reduced because of immediate contact with the newborn. Another study of forty children at a California birth center concluded that for some families sibling participation is valid, for others, it's not.

An alternative some parents consider is to bring all siblings into the birthing room immediately after the birth.

My four children (the youngest is 6) were present at the birth of our last baby. It made the baby seem more like part of the family to them, rather than an intruder, and I think it limited jealousy among the children.
Karen Gromada, Cincinnati OH

Preparing a Child to be Present at the Birth

• Take the child with you at least once for a prenatal visit. Let the child meet the doctor or midwife and listen to the baby's heartbeat or see the ultra sound.

• Enroll the child in a class designed to prepare children for watching a birth. Birth centers and hospitals with birthing rooms usually offer some sort of training appropriate to children of different ages. Remember to tell a child that going to the hospital doesn't mean anything is wrong with mom.

• Be sure the child understands all aspects of birth, including contractions, the mother's red face and sounds she may make, the breaking of the bag of waters, episiotomy, blood that will be present on the mother and the baby, that this is "extra blood" that mother doesn't need, and about the appearance of the placenta. Explain that cutting the cord does not hurt the baby, just as cutting hair and nails does not hurt the child. Prepare your child also for the appearance of a newborn—naked, the bluish color, and the white lubricant that will cover the baby's skin.

• Use books and pictures, even videos, to help with your explanations, including any pictures you have of your older child's birth or newborn period.

• Tell your child that the baby will probably cry, and that he or she will not be able to play with the baby immediately after it is born, though it might be possible to let your child place a finger into the baby's hand to "hold hands" shortly after the birth.

Around the time I was seven and one-half months pregnant, we purchased an inexpensive fetoscope, and listen-
ing to the baby's "heartbeep" became part of our bedtime
ritual. The one thing we forgot to mention was that the
umbilical cord would have to be cut. It wasn't a big thing
for Lisa, but we had forgotten to mention it and she asked
a lot of questions about the cord.

Kathy Parks, Boblingen, W. Germany

• It's important for both parents to share the desire for the older
child to attend the birth of the baby. Secondly, the child should be
interested in attending the birth without your having to do a hard
sell.

• Prepare your child (and possibly yourself) for seeing you naked by bathing together and letting him or her see you dress and undress.

• Simulate for your child the positions and facial expressions he or she may see you make during the birth and also the sound you may make. Let kids know labor is hard work!

• Let the child see and touch the equipment you assemble for a home birth and explain the uses of the clamp, scissors, suction pump, and other items.

• Mention the possibility of problems and explain that if they occur, the child will leave and the mother may go to the hospital labor room or surgical suite.

• Select one person (not the father) to be with the child throughout the entire birth process—someone who will have no responsibility for the mother or any part of the birth. This person will attend to the child's wants and needs and take him or her from the room if necessary or desired. It's advisable for the person to attend classes with the child or at least to read some of the birthing books with him or her. Choose someone who will be able to concentrate on the child throughout, and who won't get wrapped up in the excitement of the delivery and forget about the child's needs. Be sure the child understands this arrangement. That person can also encourage the child to let mom know she is doing a good job!

• Explain to your child before hand that if asked to leave the room by mom or dad, it is not because they are being rejected or that mom and dad are angry, but there are some times when mom is just going to need time out or time alone.

• Two books worth reading on the topic of children at the birth are: *Mom and Day and I Are Having a Baby!* by Maryann Malecki (Pennypress, 1982) is written specifically for a child who is expected to attend a sibling's birth. At present it is the only book available for children. It is fairly explicit with every stage of birth illustrated in anatomical detail. *Birth—Through Children's Eyes* by Sandra Van Dam Anderson & Penny Simkin (Pennypress, 1981) is a unique 140-page book written for adults to help them see how children view birth.

In the Birthing Room

• Be sure there are books, toys, games, and snacks for your child to enjoy during the "boring" times.

• Let the child know that he or she can leave the room at any time and may or may not come back, as he or she chooses. Of course, the child's support person remains with the child, and has ideas of where to go (cafeteria, nursery, waiting room, lobby or nearby park or store).

• Let the child help the mother by holding ice chips, getting her a drink, rubbing her back, or walking around the room with her. An older child can be in charge of changing records or tapes and may even be allowed to take pictures or video tapes of the birth.

Remember that children do not "fail" in any way in attending their sibling's birth, the same way that mom and her partner do not fail at giving birth, no matter what actually happens.

4

How Can I Keep My Older Child from Feeling Left Out?

Now your family is experiencing growing pains. You enjoy the feeling of competence you didn't have the first time, and you're not quite as frightened at the thought of your responsibility to the new little life, but as a mother, you're finding that there's just no way you can fully satisfy the needs of everyone. It's hard, sometimes impossible, to find time for those important private moments with your older child and with your husband. Having two (or more) children definitely means more work for you.

All you can do is your best. Time is on your side. Patience, a good sense of humor, and plenty of love will see you through. It's important to realize that kids are very adaptable. Chances are your older child is not going to suffer or carry scars from this experience, especially if you make the effort to include him or her in every phase of your adjustment to a new kind of family life. With each additional child, your family changes, and changes are seldom easy. Don't assume the child will feel instant warmth or love for the baby, and don't be too disappointed if it doesn't happen. That's asking for too much too soon. Jealousy toward a new sibling is almost universal. Don't discourage your child's invention of an imaginary playmate if it occurs at this time. Instead, appreciate it! And don't pick this particular time to try to break a pacifier or security blanket habit, either.

> **Don't worry yourself sick over the transition for children at home. I drained myself mentally the first few days, then realized that I was the one having a rough time adjusting. I always wanted to be saying and doing the right things— and no mom is perfect. Feel successful about your busy days if you have spent a little special time with each child.**
> *Vicki Pouchet, Kalamazoo, MI*

Announcing the New Arrival

• Let the child help make the phone calls to announce the baby's arrival.

• Get mints or lollypops for the child to pass around to friends. You may be able to find some with "It's a boy/girl!" printed on the wrappers, or tie pink or blue ribbons around them.

• Get your older child a T-shirt bearing the message: "I'm the Big Brother/Big Sister." (See p. 59.)

• You may want to give your older child one "super-present" to help celebrate the birth—something that shows he or she is bigger and older, such as a riding toy for a toddler, or some rather sophisticated art materials for a preschooler. (Some parents tell the child the present is from the baby, but others discourage this, because the child is smart enough to know that babies can't decide on gifts or shop for them.)

Within the Family

• Recognize the fact that you may find yourself enjoying the baby and snapping at your chatterbox toddler—almost wishing he or she would go away. Don't feel guilty! It's very normal. Some parents report just the opposite problem: the baby seems boring compared to the toddler who can do so many interesting things.

• Try to keep your older child's daily routine as normal as possible.

• Help your child understand the baby is not going to take over.

• Give him or her plenty of praise and recognition for good behavior and help.

Have You Said to Your Child Lately

"I love you."

"I'm glad *(the baby's name)* has you for a sister/ brother!"

"You are my favorite 2- (or whatever age) year-old. "
(Inappropriate if older child is a twin!)

• Remember to take as many pictures of the child as you do of the baby, and have him or her be alone in some of them. (But do remember to take many pictures of this second child, the one seen but fleetingly in family albums. One second child was convinced that she was adopted because there was no baby book for her, and few baby pictures in the family albums.)

• Make a point of having Daddy or Mommy talk to the older child first when arriving home, and then look in on the baby.

• Say, "My hands are busy right now" when your child wants attention and you're occupied with the baby. It's a little less personal than saying you're busy, and it may pacify the child.

• Try to juggle the baby's first and last feedings of the day so both children don't go to bed and get up at the same time. (Easier said than done!) Some parents are able to have breakfast alone with the older child before the baby wakes or after the baby goes back for a nap after the first feeding.

• Schedule private time with your older child. Get a sitter or leave the baby with your spouse so you can do things with the child that the baby "can't do."

• Likewise, spend time alone with the baby, too. Your older child will have to learn to share you.

After Ben's birth, Nathan went through a stage during which he liked to whisper "secrets" up close in our ears. We would whisper back such things as, "Pssst, you sure have a nice baby." He thought that was great fun. 3-year-old Nathan still considers Benjamin his baby.

Carol Reinhard, Corvallis, OR

Our 3 1/2-year-old has had many imaginary playmates. I've noticed that they change as her needs change. Since the birth of our last baby, she has a "big brother" and a "big sister." They give her attention when I'm busy.

Sarah Holback, Albers, IL

Our 3-year-old went through a very clingy stage right before the baby arrived, and I feared the worst. But when our new son was born, things went much more smoothly than I had anticipated. He was very whiny and weepy for a few days after I returned from the hospital, but the baby seemed to be exactly what he expected and he quickly perked up. The world hadn't come to an end and soon he was noticing positive things about the baby on his own.

N. Warren, Columbus, OH

• If your family celebrates big events by planting a tree or with some other symbolic gesture, be sure the older child helps—and be sure to point out how his or her birth was celebrated.

• When an activity is interrupted by the new baby let your older child know you must attend to the baby but that you will be back and you'll finish what you were doing together.

• Get a pet, if you can handle it; even a goldfish will give your child something else to focus on. On the other hand, if your oldest is under the age of 3 you may find yourself protecting the pet as well as the new baby from the affections of your older child.

While You're Feeding the Baby

Be aware that your child of preschool age or younger is very apt to feel left out at feeding time and may feel a loss of intimacy. The child is also likely to feel particularly jealous at this time.

• Make careful preparations before you start feeding the baby. Set up a table, lay out a snack for the older child, and get out the toys and books you and the child will share while you feed the baby.

• Seat yourself on the couch so you and your older child can cuddle, read, or watch TV while you're feeding the baby.

• Or sit on the floor with your child, where you can help with puzzles, games, and the like.

• If your child is too young to answer the phone for you, a cordless phone would be a good thing to buy. You won't have to jump up and answer it or let it go unanswered.

Nursing

• When possible, let Daddy spend some time with the child while you're nursing the baby.

• Let your older child try nursing again if he or she wants to and if you're comfortable about it (but only if you are). Chances are it will be a quick, somewhat embarrassed attempt. The child probably won't like the taste of your milk, won't be able to suck properly, and will lose interest quickly.

• Do your prebirth breathing exercises before nursing to help you relax and make the milk come down faster, and have your toddler or preschooler do them with you.

Bottle-Feeding

• Let your child help you hold the baby's bottle. Explain how liquid must cover the nipple area so the baby won't swallow air.

• Hold your baby when bottle-feeding, but on occasion put the baby in an infant seat so you can play with the older child and still maintain eye contact with the baby.

• Let your child bottle-feed a doll with a realistic toy bottle. Look for one that seems to empty when it's inverted. When the child "feeds" the doll, it looks like the doll is really drinking the play milk.

Other Things to Do at Baby's Feeding Time

• Play records or tapes of favorite songs.

• Record the child's voice and the sounds the baby makes.

• Let the child draw and color. (This is not the time for finger painting!)

• Get out the Viewmaster and slides.

• Read to the child, perhaps from a special book used only at nursing time. Reading at any time gives double pleasure—the baby likes the sound of your voice and the older child enjoys the attention.

• Talk about pictures in a family album.

When Visitors Come

• Stall visitors and let the older child be the center of attention for a few minutes. Tell them (but not in front of the older child) that the older child needs attention too.

• Then let him or her lead the guests to the baby's room, help you bring the baby out, or assist with serving refreshments.

• And, while refreshments are being eaten, don't be surprised if your child tells the visitors just how the baby gets his or her refreshments from inside Mommy's blouse.

• Show pictures of the older child as well as of the baby.

• Ask the child to unwrap presents brought for the baby.

• Keep a supply of little gifts on hand to give the older child if visitors don't bring something for him or her.

• Or, as some parents prefer to do, explain to the child that babies "come with nothing" and need lots of things, and that when his or her birthday comes the presents will be for the child alone.

After making certain that my 3 1/2-year-old was safely occupied, I sat down to "quietly" nurse her new brother. All went quite well and I was congratulating myself on my abilities as a mom when a little voice came from the stairway: "Mom, could you come get my gum off the wall?" Oh well, at least she doesn't hit him.
                                                    Kathleen Bricker, Ann Arbor, MI

The Shared Room

Many American parents feel that children should have their own rooms, separate from their siblings, that each child needs the privacy and space offered by a room of one's own. That's not the norm in many other countries. In fact, a lot of parents here are now opting to put their kids together, even if they don't have to. And kids don't always object. As one child put it: "You and Dad share a room. Why do I have to be alone?"

If your baby is going to share a room with a toddler, however, you may want to keep the baby in your room for the first few weeks. Be cautious about a shared room with a child under the age of three. Jealous and abusive behavior could occur in early hours when you are not yet awake.

Other reasons for keeping the baby in your room in a bassinet or carriage initially are that the older child won't be disturbed, you won't be taking a chance on the older one trying to pick up the baby, and you'll save yourself some running. On the other hand, the sooner you put the children together, the sooner they'll adjust.

• Put the crib up in the shared room a few weeks before the baby arrives to set up the scenario of the shared room.

• If the child is jealous because the baby is in your room, set up a corner of another room where the bassinet can be placed until your own bedtime.

• Consider adopting the "family bed" plan occasionally, if it's not against your inclinations. One way to stretch the space in the parents' bed is to put a crib (with one side removed) right next to the bed.

• Room sharing of siblings should begin once your infant sleeps through the night.

• Supply privacy in a shared room by setting up a screen or room divider of some kind. Bookshelves work well.

• Attach blinds to tracks on the ceiling and floor to make a more permanent separation. Or even build four- or five-foot plywood walls in a corner of the room. Pad the walls to muffle noise, and cover the padding with fabric attached with a staple gun.

• Try to supply play or study space for your older child in another part of the house so the schedules of the two children won't conflict.

• Let your baby nap in the master bedroom so the older child can use his or her bedroom for play during baby's naptime.

• Keep a sleep monitor (intercom) in the children's bedroom to hear when the baby is awakening and you can get to the baby before the older child is disturbed.

• Put the sounder sleeper to bed first.

Some parents make few accommodations and still find that children adjust. Babies get used to sleeping anywhere and toddlers learn to sleep through wakenings and diaper changes.

In *The Family Bed* by Tine Thevenin, the author discusses how children who grow up in a "family bed" often wean from sleeping with the parents by sleeping with siblings. Here children not only share a room but also share a bed!

Childproofing the Shared Room

• Take every precaution you can to protect the baby from the physical attentions of your toddler, even loving, well intentioned ones. Set the crib mattress at its lowest point and leave the crib side up at all times.

• Remove any furniture (stools, etc.) that your toddler could use to climb into the crib.

• Try to get the baby up in the morning before the older child wakes, or put him or her down at night after the older one is asleep. And try to keep afternoon nap times separate.

• Keep an intercom in the room so you know who is in there if you can't be for the moment.

• Put away, for a time, toys with small parts that your older child might try to share with the baby. At least keep such toys in another part of the house.

• Later, when the baby is mobile and curious, give your older child a feeling of control by supplying locks for a few drawers in which precious and/or dangerous objects can be kept.

• Create private play space by carpeting a closet you can spare.

A Sibling Library

These books can help prepare a child for life with a new sibling. They describe feelings that children can come to understand are normal, and they provide expectations of life with a new baby.

Feel free to use your child's name instead of the one assigned by the book, if you think the story will be enhanced by this tip.

The New Baby at Your House
by Joanna Cole
William Morrow & Co., 1985

Lovely black-and-white photographs of a variety of different
families and siblings record the
arrival of a new baby. The text is
supportive and reassuring for
new brothers and sisters, describing in honest, positive terms
what life is like when a new
baby joins the family.

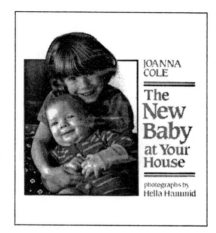

The New Baby
by Fred Rogers
A Mister Roger's
  Neighborhood Book
Putnam, 1985

In this full color, photo book,
simple, reassuring captions talk
about different feelings and
happenings that occur when a
new baby enters a family. The
photos show various siblings—
sisters and brothers—rather than
just one child's point of view.

That New Baby
by Sarah B. Stein
Walker & Co., 1974

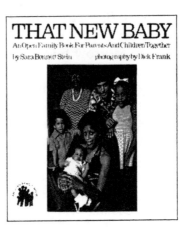

A lovely black-and-white photo essay that offers side-by-side copy for the adult and the child. This book is special in that it depicts a black family with their new baby. The feelings and the problems are the same—only the cultural models are different.

Let Me Tell You About My Baby
by Roslyn Banish
Harper and Row, 1982

This is a black-and-white photo essay from a child's perspective about the coming birth of a sibling. There is little birth and reproductive information but lots of excitement, warmth, and tenderness as the family goes through the changes brought about by the coming of a new baby. Feelings expressed include love, jealousy, joy, insecurity, and pride.

A New Baby at KoKo Bear's House
by Vicki Lansky
Illustrated by Jane Prince
The Book Peddlers, 1987

KoKo, a delightful unisex bear, goes through the family's stages of pregnancy and birth in a charmingly illustrated read-aloud book. KoKo feels bad when the gift from Aunt Beartrice is for the new baby. The text explains the key issues a child encounters and additional tips for parents are on each page.

The Berenstain Bears' New Baby
by Stan & Jan Berenstain
Random House, 1974

In typical Berenstain fashion, this illustrated paperback tells how Small Bear has outgrown his snug little bed. Papa builds him a new one just in time for the arrival of his new baby sister and he proudly stretches out in his new, bigger bed. This is also available as a book and cassette package.

There are many more storybooks about the arrival of a sibling. Several have become classics. If you want to ask for some by name from your local bookstore or library, consider these:

Books for a Younger Child

• *Mom's Home,* Jan Ormerod (Lothrop, Lee & Shepard, 1987). In this nearly wordless book, a pregnant mother takes time out to share a private moment with her toddler.

• *The Baby,* John Burningham (Crowell, 1986). A little boy describes his feelings about the new baby in the house.

• *It's Not Fair!* Anita Harper (Putnam, 1986). A young kangaroo lists her grievances during baby's first days, then gradually sees that being older has its advantages.

• *101 Things To Do With a New Baby,* Jan Ormerod (Puffin, 1984). A picture book from the view of a six year old sister with baby in their daily activities.

• *Brothers and Sisters* (Checkerboard Press, 1989). A board book of pictures of siblings playing together, eating together, etc.

• *The Trouble With Babies,* Angie and Chris Sage (Viking, 1990). An older sister shares the "trouble" as well as the good things about having a new baby.

• *Welcome, Little Baby,* Aliki (Greenwillow, 1987). This is a picture book showing a baby doing typical things with a warm, delicate touch.

Books for a Little Older Child

• *Sharing*, Nanette Newman (Doubleday, 1990). Amy is worried that her new baby brother will monopolize her parents' time.

• *Big Like Me*, Anna Grossnickle Hines (Greenwillow, 1989). "I'm going to show you everything," says the big brother to his new sibling. And, indeed, he is the perfect guide to the child's first year.

• *A Baby Sister for Frances*, Russell & Lillian Hoban (Harper & Row, 1976). Frances, a badger, decides to run away because everyone is busy looking after the baby. She doesn't run very far, and soon discovers that living by herself isn't so nice after all.

• *Betsy's Baby Brother*, Gunilla Wolde (Random House, 1975). Betsy helps take care of her little brother.

• *Peter's New Chair*, Ezra J. Keats (Harper & Row, 1967). Peter grabs his little chair before it can become one of his new sister's possessions. He finds he doesn't fit into it anymore and gives it up--even promising to help with the painting.

• *When the New Baby Comes, I'm Moving Out*, Martha Alexander (Dial, 1979). Oliver decides he'll leave home when the new baby arrives, but after a talk with Mom he thinks it might be okay to stay and be a big brother.

• *Nobody Asked Me if I Wanted a Baby Sister*, Martha Alexander (Dial, 1971). The baby has arrived and Oliver tries to get rid of her, until a clever girl makes him feel loved and wanted by his new sister.

- *I'll Fix Anthony*, Judith Viorst (Harper & Row, 1969). A little brother thinks of ways to someday get revenge on his older brother.

- *The Knee-Baby*, Mary Jarrell (Farrar, Straus & Giroux, 1973). When a new baby arrives, the old baby is relegated from his mother's lap to her knee. Jealousy is sweetly and humorously handled here.

- *Arthur's Baby*, Marc Brown (Little, Brown, 1990). Arthur becomes a resident babysitter as he confronts the trials and tribulations of having a new sister.

- *Waiting for Baby Joe*, Pat Lowery Collings (A. Whitman, 1990). Missy is confused when her brother is born almost two months early.

- *Angel's Mother's Baby*, Judy Delton (Houghton-Mifflin, 1989). Angel, who has an older brother, learns that her mother is having a baby. Suddenly everything is more complicated for this soon-to-be a middle child.

- *Baby, Come Out!* Fran Manuskin (Harper & Row, 1972). An amusing picture book shows a full-grown baby in-utero who doesn't want to come out, but eventually does, to everyone's delight.

- *One Sister Too Many*, C.S. Adler (Macmillan, 1989). A 12-year-old girl and middle child has to deal with a colicky baby in the family and a new babysitter.

- *On Mother's Lap*, Scott Michael (McGraw Hill, 1972). A young eskimo boy discovers that even with a new baby there is still room for everyone on mother's lap.

Shared Memories

My New Baby and Me:
A First Year Record Book for
Big Brothers & Sisters
by Dian G. Smith
Met. Museum/Scribners, 1986

In a large format, quality paperback, this colorful book has spaces for following "my" baby's development and milestones. It offers a cooperative venture for parents and older siblings and insures that the second baby's history is recorded.

Dress for Success!

In Short-Sleeved Cotton T-shirts that say:

"I'm the Big Brother"

"I'm the Big Sister"

Blue: S(2-4) M(4-6) L(6-8)   Pink: S(2-4) M(4-6) L(6-8)
Price: $12 plus $3 postage from PRACTICAL PARENTING
Dept. 2B, Deephaven, MN 55391 or call (800) 255-3379 (MC/V)

Turning on to Sibling Video

"Hey, What About Me?"
A Video Guide for
Brothers and Sisters
of New Babies

Kidvidz
618 Centre Street
Newton, MA 02158
(617) 243-7611

This is a delightful 25 minute video created for 2 to 6-year-olds showing real siblings with babies that kids can identify with. The kids on camera are fun to watch. It features games, lullabies and bouncing rhymes to do with babies. Feelings of anger and loneliness are handled nicely.

A Club for Your Soon-To-Be-Sibling

Siblings Forever Fan Club
401 East 86th Street, #20S
New York, New York 10028
(212) 860-7423

As a one time gift your child receives an official big brother/sister certificate, a fan club card, a Siblings Forever T-Shirt plus a handwritten note congratulating the older child on his or her new family status. A three-month membership gift includes all of the above plus something new every 2 1/2 weeks: stickers, the book *My New Baby and Me*, a bookmark, a club tote bag, and a "Hold Me" card (for your child to show friends a picture of themselves and the new baby) .

5

How Can I Get My Jealous Older Child to Accept (or Even Like!) the Baby?

If you really wanted to avoid sibling rivalry altogether, you wouldn't have a second child—having just one is the only way to avoid the problem! Too late now, so consider these things.

Your first child has had you all to himself or herself, as no other child ever will, so it's not surprising if some negative feelings toward the intruder develop. The experience of having a sibling thrust on one has been likened to that of a wife whose husband brings home a second spouse, saying, "I love you so much that I want another one like you."

It's best to follow your older child's lead, letting the sibling relationship develop at its own pace. While it's not unusual for an older child to hang over an infant, fascinated with every detail, it's also normal for him or her to show only minimal interest or even hostility. Neither attitude predicts the future sibling relationship.

Wise parents don't ignore jealousy, and they don't panic if they see it developing. They acknowledge it, letting the child know it's an emotion that's all right to have. They're understanding and patient, but they do not let the child dictate the household rules. Remember that you're the "boss." Punish when necessary, lay down your rules, and don't explain everything a dozen times. Five minutes of your time, however, when a child needs it can be more beneficial than an hour when it's convenient for you.

The best way to deal with problem behaviors is to provide some one-on-one time with your older child. Children will get your attention if they are having a hard time adjusting. Negative attention beats no attention at all. As hard as it is, try to make some special time for that new big brother or sister when there will be no interruptions. If necessary take your phone off the hook for ten or twenty minutes.

Love Can Be Shared

Show your older child in a lovely and concrete way how your love can be shared with the new baby without in any way being lessened for him or her.

Set out three candles. The first represents Mom and Dad, the second is the older child, and the third is the new baby. Light the first candle. The flame represents love. With the first candle, light the second, and then the third. Like the flames, the love is separate yet equal for all. Lighting the third candle in no way diminishes the flame of the second.

Above all, don't try to equate "fair" with "equal." Your older child must understand from the beginning that the one who needs it most will get the attention—and that right now, the baby is going to need a great deal. And don't try to be so fair with your attention that you leave out someone important: yourself!

Sometimes a child is afraid to show these natural feelings of jealousy fearing a loss of the parents' love. All siblings will feel some jealousy, and all siblings need the chance to have their feelings recognized and expressed.

Jealousy in a Child 2 1/2 or Under

The younger a child is, the less ready he or she will be to share and enjoy the new baby. A toddler this age has held the firm belief that parents exist for him or her alone, and that belief has been shattered. It's a fine point, but some experts say that what a child this age feels is more nearly envy than jealousy; he or she is envious of the attention the baby is getting. The child needs careful watching; "conscience" is not yet developed and it won't bother the child in the least to hurt the baby. His or her attitude may be: "take the baby back—get rid of it!" whether or not the thought can be put into words. The child needs understanding, but your response, expressed without threats, should be, "You don't have to like the baby, but you can't hurt the baby!"

> **I had to wheel my newborn from room to room in a buggy to protect him from my 2-year-old. (You would have had to know my 2-year-old to understand why!)**
> *Jill Heasley, Fresno, CA*

Jealousy in a 3-Year-Old

Your 3-year-old can suffer from two conflicting responses to having a sibling: the desire to be a baby, small and weak and cared for, and the desire to be big and strong and independent. The child may swing between regression (resuming habits long outgrown) and anger about having some independence thwarted by the baby's needs and demands. Your child may be angry at you for his or her "dethroning," and may even refuse to talk to you sometimes. He or she may also be wary of showing the anger for fear of losing you altogether, being "extra good" and denying feelings by turning them inward. And while he or she knows better by now, the child may take out that anger on the baby, with too-hard pats and squeezes and surreptitious pinches. Be aware that the anger may also be taken out on the family pet, in observance of the pecking order.

Jealousy in a 4- or 5-Year-Old

Your preschooler of 4 or 5, capable now of exercising self-control and understanding fully that the baby is here to stay, may have the feeling that he or she is unloved, rejected by you. The child wants to be grown-up and may demonstrate this by a lot of "watch me, see how big/strong/clever I am" activities and other thinly disguised bids for attention. He or she doesn't want to share the parents with an infant that does "disgusting things" and takes up so much time. The child may be very jealous of attention that the same-sex parent gives the baby and may compensate by focusing on the opposite-sex parent, i.e., if Suzi has lost Mom's undivided attention, Daddy belongs to her. Or a child may single out a grandparent or special adult friend for a possessive relationship. Disappointment may be one of the child's emotions, too: the baby is the wrong sex, can't do anything, and is just a nuisance. Don't worry about giving the child ideas when you make statements about his or her feelings, such as "You wish you were the only one again," or "You don't like my having to spend so much time with the baby, do you?" The feelings are there, and talking about them should help. Try creating a "family" of sock dolls to help your child verbalize feelings about family roles.

Jealousy in School-Age Children

Your school-age child may show some of the reactions of a 4 or 5-year-old, such as appearing to be at ease with the baby while holding back real feelings or showing exaggerated and insincere affection for the infant. This child, however, has interests of his or her own and capabilities that are obviously far superior to those of the baby. He or she may be jealous and somewhat resentful, but may also be proud to have a baby in the family, something that makes him or her a bit of a celebrity with peers in the neighborhood and at school.

Jealousy in Preteens and Teens

Your preteen or teenager is likely to have no feelings of jealousy or resentment at all; his or her life is full and busy. Some kids this age do feel a bit of embarrassment that their "old" parents have reproduced. And a girl of this age might be afraid that people will think the baby is hers if she's seen caring for the infant alone. Most of these older kids, though, look on the baby as a joy, an amusing and lovable live plaything. Later, when the baby becomes a toddler and gets into their things, the trouble may start.

> **I think our 3 1/2-year-old is back talking us mainly because of jealousy of a little brother who moves around in her territory now. A lot of love and setting a good example are important, though they haven't solved our problem.**
> *Nancy Loge, Wilmar, MN*

While studies and experience teach us that violence between siblings is the most frequent type of aggression in our society, it should help you to know that it is not based on the fear of losing a parent's affection or favors as children get older.

Research by Richard Felson in 1983 at the State University of New York (Albany) suggests that sibling rivalry is more mundane than psychological. It evolves around competition over use and acquisition (not ownership) of "stuff." By teen years closeness in age and sex were minimal factors.

The way parents intervene in kids' squabbles either reduces competition or makes it worse. Parents' mediation in fights appears to increase aggression. In other words, kids were more willing to fight when they could count on their parents interference. Parents, it seems, have a better chance of achieving peace when they work on house rules and parameters that prevent them from playing referee.

Helping Children Handle Their Feelings of Jealousy

• Admit to your child that the baby can be a nuisance; express your own occasional annoyance, but don't ever apologize for the baby's existence.

• Let your baby "wait" once in a while when you're finishing up something with your older child.

• Give your older child new privileges—a later bedtime, increased allowance, special activities—now that he or she is a big brother or big sister. This may be the time to start letting a preschooler play outdoors alone—a great "grown-up" activity—if circumstances are just right.

• Be sensitive if your child doesn't particularly like the role of big brother or sister thrust upon him or her. "Yes, sometimes it's hard to be the big brother/sister."

• Provide some out-of-home experiences for a young child. A 2- to 3-year-old may like the idea of a regular play group, or have special personal experiences like going to the zoo with a babysitter. This should not be done, however, if you are trying to get the child out of the way, or if the child interprets the event as such.

• Don't make your child feel guilty about feeling jealous. He or she can't control these feelings.

• Don't tell your child how to feel. Let your child tell you how he or she feels. Acknowledge those feelings. "I hear you're feeling unhappy about the baby."

• Point out the fact that someday he or she might be a mother or father too, and may have an older one and a baby just as you do.

> **Be patient. Our 3-year-old was quite jealous when our little girl was born. We let her help out as much as possible. A year later, they are the best of friends.**
> *Chris Rohret, Tiffin, IA*

• Stress how the baby loves or enjoys having an older brother or sister. "See how Jennifer smiles when she sees you. She thinks you are very special."

• Stagger naps and feedings so you can be alone with the older child sometimes.

• Look at old pictures together, especially those that show you doing the things with and for the older child that you now do for the baby.

• Let a child overhear you telling another adult how helpful and kind he or she is with the baby. Direct praise, unfortunately, is sometimes perceived as a "con job," which it may very well be.

• Say "I love you" often—without adding, "and the baby, too."

Second-Stage Jealousy: When the Baby Becomes Mobile!

Right now, you're thinking only of the immediate acceptance of your new baby by your older child. Sibling rivalry does go on, though, sometimes into adulthood. You might as well accept the fact that you'll be reading, hearing, and talking about jealousy—and living with it—for a long time to come.

Once your infant is mobile, your concerns with sibling rivalry will center on protecting the older child's possessions and "space," and, just as important, his or her place in the family.

• Teach your older child that the baby who grabs things will be easily distracted by a quick gift of something else. (A sibling under the age of 2 will not comprehend this "trick. ")

• Don't make an issue out of sharing. Just give positive strokes for being able to engage in a wider range of play. The abstract concept of ownership and sharing are simply beyond the understanding of a 2 1/2 year old.

• And explain that a baby who grabs (toys, hair, etc.) is simply exploring a new world and doesn't understand "mine vs. yours" or how his or her actions hurt others.

• Encourage the older child to minimize problems by keeping his or her things up high or safely put away.

• Provide locks and keys for boxes and drawers to help the older child protect precious items.

• Be sensitive to baby items and toys passed "down" to the baby. The older child might decide to reclaim a blanket or toy to protect his or her status if feeling threatened.

• Get an extra baby gate for the door to your older child's room to keep the baby out.

• Let your older child play in the baby's playpen with his or her own things.

• Continue to avoid focusing too much attention on the baby of the family in the presence of the older child. If friends and relatives persist, draw attention to the older one's abilities and achievements in any way you can. Don't stress the "mother's helper with the baby" aspect after the first few months.

• Go through your older child's toys and put away what isn't played with. Bring them out later as the baby's toys.

• Ask your older child to chose some toys the baby can play with from his or her collection. A toddler often enjoys taking "control" of the baby's play. Control is often shown by being overprotective of the baby or by becoming mom's best baby helper.

• Be sure the older child gets his or her fair share of attention, love, and praise within the family circle too.

• Make and observe a few house rules to ensure the physical safety of the younger child, but don't overprotect him or her. You'll be setting up a situation for resentment.

Regression in Young Children

Be aware that regressive behavior can occur at a week, a month, at seven months (most common), or even longer after the arrival of a second baby. It is normal. Don't punish it or you might reinforce the child's feelings about being bad or unwanted. Be patient, and don't overlook your child's needs at this trying time.

• Be aware that a young child's return to babyish habits in such matters as toilet training, eating or dressing, and baby talk may or may not be a sign of jealousy; it may simply reflect stress.

• Treat regressive behavior (especially if it's wetting or dirtying pants) without punishment and using non-judgmental language. A return to diapers can be done matter-of-factly.

• Remember that being a baby is, to a child, the key to getting a parent's attention, and regression seems to be a way to compete on the baby's own terms. Your child may be genuinely confused about why certain behavior (thumbsucking, wetting pants) is bad when he or she does it, and acceptable or even good when the baby does it.

• Consider indulging regressive behavior to help a child work through it. Try changing his or her clothes on the changing table—even adding a sprinkle of baby powder, or serving all table liquids in a bottle.

• Don't scold or criticize your child. Instead, make an effort to show him or her your care and love and tell the child how lucky the baby is to have a big sibling.

• Praise generously any mature behavior you can spot, and point out the many advantages of being older and more grown-up.

• Encourage grandparents or other relatives to offer your regressing child special consideration and attention.

• If your child is in day care or nursery school, he or she is probably showing regressive behavior there, too. Talk to the caregiver or teacher about helping the child handle jealousy. Some schools have special celebrations to mark the transition to big-brother or big-sister status.

My 3-year-old son seemed to love his new little sister, but I guess I knew that he was kidding himself when he gave up walking for a few days and started to crawl again, just when she did.

Roz Nemer, Minnetonka, MN

"I Almost Had a Heart Attack"

Once I heard the baby make a strange noise. I turned around to see my 2-year-old standing on my 2-month-old baby's stomach! No permanent harm was done, but I almost had a heart attack!

Becky Wilkins, Lubbock, TX

Mother hears splash from bathroom, runs to investigate. There stands 2 1/2-year-old on floor, 1 year-old with feet in toilet. 2-year-old: "He looked like he wanted to take a little swim!"

Kay Coburn-Dyer, Bloomington, MN

Our 3-year-old had developed a game with her father. She would "hide" under a pillow, and he would search for her. I came back from the door one day to find her holding the pillow over her 4 month-old sister's face as the little one struggled for breath. I overreacted and pushed her away. Finally, sobbing, she told me she had been teaching the baby to hide, not trying to hurt her.

P. M. Dash, Marietta, GA

One day when Rebecca was only a few weeks old, my 5-year-old son decided she should be sleeping on the couch. He plucked her from her bassinet and walked toward the couch. I entered the room, and my son—caught red-handed—decided to get rid of the evidence. He was too far from the bassinet, so he tossed her toward the sofa, about three feet away. It could only have been an act of God that Rebecca actually landed "safely"—still asleep!

Robyn Neuman, Beaver Dam, WI

"Big Kids" Can Help

• Let a toddler watch proceedings at the dressing table from a stool, handing you items you need and helping pat the baby dry after a bath.

• Wear an apron with big pockets to store baby accessories in, and take out just one at a time to avoid more help than you need.

• Let the child fetch and carry for you around the house, sort the baby's laundry, or help burp the baby.

• Allow the child to hold the baby on a pillow, in a big chair, when you are in the room to supervise. Don't hover nervously or take the baby away at the first opportunity. Your older child will get the impression that you don't trust him or her.

• Do put the baby safely in the infant seat inside the playpen if you leave the room even for a minute. And set the crib mattress at its lowest point so you won't get "help" in picking up the infant.

• Be aware that the baby's soft spot, at the top of the head, is protected by a firm muscle. Don't overreact when your child inadvertently (?) touches that area, which you've just explained is delicate and to be avoided.

• Remember that a preschooler's or young child's willingness to help may exceed his or her ability to do so. Both baby and child must be protected. Be available to supervise any holding or feeding and don't entrust the baby to the child's care alone for any extended period of time.

• Accept help from even a quite young child with the baby book and photo album and take advantage of the opportunity to talk about the older child's baby years.

• Let a child help pick out baby food in the grocery store and other items you may need for the baby.

Don't be overprotective. Hovering over the baby with too many restrictions only suggests inappropriate behavior. We let our son experiment, within reason, and learn for himself what his sister did and didn't like.
Jodi Junge, Huntingdon Valley, CA

I have to admit this was one area in which I failed miserably. I was so afraid of my 3-year-old hurting the baby, I discouraged togetherness. I wish I could have done it differently.
Linda Merry, St. Louis Park, MN

• Encourage the child to be a teacher by showing the baby (once past infancy) how to drink from a cup, to crawl, walk, draw, etc.

• Let an older child make up and record a message for the phone-answering machine: "Mom's busy with the baby; the best time to call is around four o'clock" (or whenever).

• Welcome the real help a preteen or teenager can give you, but try not to overdo requests for it so resentment won't build up.

• Treat your baby-sitting older child with the same consideration you do an outsider, whether or not you pay for the service.

Playing With Baby

• Put the child's finger in the baby's palm and show your own delight when the baby clenches it.

• Show your child how to test the baby's sucking reflex by putting the back of the child's hand on the baby's mouth or touching the baby's lower lip gently with a finger.

• Show the child how to get the baby to turn his or her head by having the child gently stroke one of the baby's cheeks or shake a rattle near the baby's head.

• Let your child join in the infant games you play with the baby, such as *Pat-a-Cake* and *This Little Piggy*. And explain that the baby will be interested in any game for only a few minutes at a time.

• Stimulate both children by exposing them to different odors, such as those of vanilla, peanut butter, and coffee. Enjoy the baby's reactions with your older child.

• Reinforce the baby's responsiveness to the older sibling. "Look how happy your baby brother becomes when you sing to him."

Problems were insignificant until 9-month-old sister "got into her stuff." They fought then and two years later they're still fighting!

D. Schipani, Ellicott City, MD

Teaching Gentleness

• Start before the baby is born by encouraging your child to practice being gentle with your pet, or a doll or stuffed animal. Use the doll to show your child how to hold a baby correctly, supporting the back and neck. That way, you won't have to constantly correct your child when the baby arrives.

• Continue the practice by having the child hold and care for a doll while you do the same for the baby.

• Talk a lot about the need for gentleness, explaining that little babies "hurt easier" than big kids do.

• Be gentle yourself, with both children. Your example will be the best teacher.

• Speak calmly and quietly. Don't yell "Stop!" or "Careful!" however much you may be tempted to—and you will be tempted.

• And take comfort in the fact that babies are surprisingly tough and resilient. (Don't leave them unattended, but don't give your older child the feeling that you're watching him or her like a hawk, either.)

• Reinforce the gentle behavior your older child does display. "I like how you hold your baby brother so gently," or "Hold her hand gently, that's right."

In retrospect, I found it was I who should have been better prepared. I perpetuated Brian's aggressive responses (hitting, ripping, breaking toys) by my own extreme concern for his hurt feelings. He sensed my sympathy and tested me beyond what was called for. I was so worried about him that I went so far as not to snuggle the baby when he was around.

Wendy Short, Bethel Park, PA

Helping Your Child Handle Anger

Your older child may be angry—very angry—with you for bringing home this intruder. He or she may be afraid to show this anger, so you should watch carefully for signs of it. One 3-year-old thinly disguised his anger with what he thought was humor, calling his mother "the big nipple." Another made no such attempt and simply walked up to his mother and gave her a swift kick in the shin while she was nursing the baby. Yet another family used a toy telephone to great advantage during this stage. The child used the telephone to express negative feelings about the baby ("Doctor, the baby is dying! Come and take him back to the hospital!"). The telephone allowed the child to get the feelings out safely, because everyone was aware that it was all "just pretend." Give your toddler or preschooler as many opportunities as possible to vent anger in acceptable ways.

One caution: A toddler may handle a baby awkwardly and even hurt the child unintentionally. Be sure to distinguish between this and a deliberate attempt to cause pain.

• Encourage physical activity to work off anger: running around outside, punching a mattress, or throwing stones into a pond. All these can use up angry energy.

• Or try a punching toy, or a family of sock dolls (the child can even help you sew or draw on facial features and expressions) or stuffed animals that can be thrown around, hit, talked to, or punished.

• State plainly that it's okay for the child to be angry with you—you're angry with him or her sometimes too—but that it's not okay to hit or kick Mom or the baby. "We don't hurt anyone no matter how we feel. I don't let anyone hurt you and I won't let anyone hurt the baby."

• Use aggressive behavior directed at you, the parent, to help a child attach words to his or her negative behavior: "Are you angry with me because I gave the baby so much attention today? I can understand how you wouldn't feel good about that. What can you and I do special tonight (read a book) or tomorrow (go to the park)?"

• Teach your child to express anger verbally: "I'm mad at you because . . ." and then talk about the feelings. Very young children can't do this effectively (they're better at tantrums) and some older children have a harder time with this technique than others.

• If you're a working mother on maternity leave, your older child is enjoying a bonus of your attention, but be aware that he or she may also be thinking, "She stays home for the baby, but not for me." A little explaining may be in order.

• Remind yourself, when your child is venting anger, that it's best that the negative feelings come out rather than remain hidden.

Behavioral Warning Signs

It is time to look into counseling when your child persistently:

- avoids or ignores the baby and is unable to show the baby any affection

- is consistently angry, taunting and aggressive towards the baby

- is overly good or caring with the baby yet still has nightmares and sleeping difficulty

6

How Can I Help My Child Handle Special Circumstances?

It's impossible to predict many of the special circumstances that may surround a birth, although some—adoption, for example, or perhaps a cesarean birth—are known about in advance. If you do know that something will be different, you'll prepare your older child as best you can. Otherwise, you'll take what comes as a family—learning, adjusting, and perhaps suffering together.

If You're Adopting a Baby

• Familiarize your child with the details of reproduction and birth just as you would if you were giving birth. Be sure that he or she, especially if quite young, understands that the baby does not come out of nowhere and has been, or will be, born like any other baby.

• Pay special attention to actual or implied questions as to why you're making this special effort to add to your family. Having

Adapting to Adoption

Many groups that help with adoption also offer help in family and sibling adjustment.

Adoptive Families of America is an organization that helps adoptive parents, including those with transracial, foreign, handicapped, abused, and older children. They will supply information about local support groups in most states, and they provide a 65-page bimonthly newsletter ($13/year). (Formerly OURS.)

> Adoptive Families of America
> 3307 Hwy. 100 North
> Minneapolis, MN 55422
> 612-535-4829

Adoptive Parents Education Program will send you information with a SASE for 45 cents. They provide a newsletter, referral and information.

> Adoptive Parents Education Program
> PO 32114
> Phoenix, AZ 85064
> 602-957-2896

a baby is one thing; going out to search for one may be harder to explain, and harder for your child to understand.

• Explain to the child old enough to ask why a mother would not want her own baby, that the baby's parents couldn't give it the proper love and care and knew it was best for the baby to have a loving family raise him or her.

• Take advantage of any classes or other informational sources offered by your adoption agency that will help your child understand adoption.

• Let your child participate as fully as possible in the adoption procedures: looking at pictures of the baby, going with you to pick up the baby, and if older, being present at legal proceedings.

• Study together the culture of a foreign-born adoptee, preparing your child as well as yourself for differences and for adjustments that you'll all have to make.

• Celebrate the adoption as you would a birth, including the extended family and friends. Let your older child participate as much as possible in arrangements.

• Recognize that resentments expressed by your own child are to be expected (after the initial excitement and newness wears off) but are not necessarily to be attributed to adoption. The process of being displaced and having to share family affections is hard on any sibling. A normal response of "take the baby back" should be your cue to give the older child extra, individualized attention.

Arrival of a New Baby
When There is an Adopted Child

•Like all children, an adopted child will feel insecure and displaced by a new brother or sister.

•Realize it's normal if you feel the need to protect your older adopted child from experiencing feelings of abandonment of the biological mother.

•You are entitled to enlarge the size of your family without feeling guilty.

•All children experience sibling rivalry but don't allow bullying or entitlement based on claims of adoption or biological superiority.

Best Books to Look For

While books mentioned elsewhere in this book are going to be useful, you may specifically want to get:

•*Susan and Gordon Adopt a Baby*, Judy Freudberg and Tony Geiss (Random House/CTW, 1986). This chronicles the day on Sesame Street when Susan and Gordon adopt baby Miles and Big Bird is jealous but learns that there is enough love for everyone.

•*Twice Upon A Time: Born & Adopted*, Eleanora Patterson. (EP Press, Brattleboro, VT, 1987). This covers conception, birth and adoption.

> Our 7-year-old only child knew for almost three years that he was getting a sister. (We had applied to adopt a baby.) What he did not know was that she would be a year old and could talk and get into his stuff right away. We did much to prepare him and ourselves but it still was not enough. I guess the best thing we did was take a trip shortly before we got her so we could have that time together before the new one came. It would have helped if we had realized how much this new addition would change our lives.
>
> *Marcia Ashodian, Fresno, CA*

If You're Having a C-Section

• Explain to your child, if you know or suspect that you'll be having a C-section, the differences between cesarean and natural birth. If the child is old enough to understand, you can go into detail about your birth canal being small or the baby's need to "get out" faster than a normal birth would allow.

• Take the opportunity to prepare a child for your need to stay in the hospital longer than normal, and the fact that you'll require extra rest and reduced activity for a while after you get home.

• If you have a toddler, make a playpen of your bed when you get home, keeping playthings and books within reach.

• Use your foot as a lever to raise your toddler to you when sitting down, instead of leaning down to pick him or her up.

Books on Cesarean Delivery

Daniel's Question:
A Cesarean Birth Story
By Elaine Sussman Allinson
Willow Tree Press, 1981
(914) 354-9139

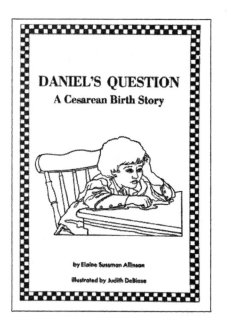

The details of cesarean delivery can be frightening for a young child. This nice little booklet presents the facts in a simple, satisfying way. A mother tells her young son how his birth was "special" and different from that of his friend. Nice line drawings move the story along for young children.

For Adults

• *The Cesarean Birth Experience*, Bonnie Donovan (Beacon Press, 1985). Practical, comprehensive and reassuring guide to family-centered cesarean birth.

• *Silent Knife: Cesarean Prevention and VBAC*, Nancy Cohen & Estner (Bergin & Garvey, 1983). Powerful, thoroughly documented critique of the growing reliance on cesarean.

• *The VBAC Experience*, Lynn Richards (Bergin & Garvey, 1987). Covers a wide range of birthing issues through birth stories by parents and professionals.

If the New Baby is a Half-Sibling

Each situation is different because of the variations possible here, i.e. natural mother or stepmother having the new baby; age of child; primary residence of the child. Regardless of the details, there are some things you can do to make the adjustment easier:

• Be aware that a child who has been pleased with a marriage and stepparent will not necessarily be thrilled with a new sibling. It's one thing to add a stepmom or stepdad and quite another to add a new child. It's direct competition for affection!

• Try to see the situation from a child's viewpoint. It looks like there is only so much love to go around. While a child might have complete love from each natural parent in each separate household, the addition of a baby in one of those homes may be perceived by the child as making only half as much love available.

• It's true that an "ours" child can bring siblings from different households together because they now share a blood relative. But don't burden the new child with the responsibility of unifying the family, especially as that child gets older.

• Remember that a child moving between households will be party to feelings of the other parent who may not be thrilled (and may even be angry) about this new arrival.

• Let a child express the feelings that are pushing and pulling him or her and don't judge or deny or say that he or she "shouldn't" feel that way. Feelings are real. Accept them first, and give them time to change.

• Do everything you can to help grandparents and other relatives accept the new baby as part of the extended family and to demonstrate their acceptance of the older half siblings.

• Point out examples of half siblings in families of friends and relatives if you can. Older children may be surprised to find that they have lots of company.

> **When my visiting stepson's mother became pregnant, he was visibly upset—came around for lots of snuggles on the couch, wanted (for the first time) to call me "Mom," turned a deaf ear on anything to do with babies. When his father's and my new baby was announced a year or so later, he took it all in stride. (P.S. He's just great with both little brothers now.)**
>
> *T. Burbank, New York, NY*

• Be sensitive to the fact that this is one more change for a child who has already been through a lot of change. Don't be disappointed or surprised if the news of a baby on the way is met with a less than joyous response.

• Your child will probably have a lot of questions that he or she may not feel free to ask. Try to anticipate them and provide honest answers. Will the family be moving (again) to make room for the baby? What will the baby's last name be? Is a half sibling as good as a "whole" sibling? Will they like the baby better than they like me?

• Be aware that if your child has been secretly hoping that his or he real parents will get back together, the presence of a baby may dash those hopes forever. This could be yet another reason for the child to resent (or even hate) the baby.

• If the stress of pregnancy or the new baby causes friction between you and your spouse, reassure your older child that it doesn't mean another divorce is imminent. In fact, your decision to have the baby can be evidence that you believe the marriage will last.

• Be prepared for the possibility that the new baby may also cause jealousy between parents: "Does he/she love this baby more than he/she loves my child?" Discuss these feelings openly and honestly with your spouse, and try not to involve your child if possible.

Help for Keeping In Step

The Step Family Foundation, Inc.
333 West End Ave.
New York, NY 10023
212-877-3244
Provides information about regional groups, organizes lectures and publishes a newsletter.

Stepfamily Association of America
602 E. Joppa Road
Baltimore, MD 21204
301-823-7570
Offers information and books on stepparenting.

If You're Having Two (or More)

If your new arrival turns out to be two instead of one, be sure to turn to your local parents-of-twins support group at once. You need the advice and support right from the start, so don't waste any time getting it. Your doctor or a nurse at the hospital may be able to help you find a group, or write to: National Organization of Mothers of Twins Club, 12404 Princess Jeanne NE, Albuquerque, NM 87112.

With an older singleton at home, be aware that his or her problems in trying to deal with the arrival of twins will be greater than if you had brought home only one baby. In fact, if the twins are the first born, they will suffer less displacement with the arrival of a new baby because they have each other to turn to. Not only is the older child displaced, but by two, no less. Mother and Father are more tired and busy. Friends and family are even more intrigued by twins. It is very easy for an older child to get lost in those first few weeks and become resentful.

• Don't be surprised by regressive, jealous, or angry behavior. It's normal and it's better if it's expressed rather than repressed. (Of course, it's not fun to deal with, especially because the double duty of twins will be draining your energy at the same time.) Listen to and don't chastise negative feelings that are expressed.

• Don't emphasize any change in routine or curtailment of family activities as being the fault of the twins. This will only increase your child's resentment.

• Affirm your older child's place in the family as the big brother/big sister. Generously praise any helpfulness.

• Remember that the children are all equally brothers and sisters. Don't divide them into "the twins" and the "other" children.

• Make an effort to set aside private one-on-one time for the older child, even if it means hiring two baby-sitters for the twins while you and your older child go out for an hour or so.

> **Introducing our newborn twins to my 3- and 5-year-old was the hardest part for me. I knew it would be difficult, but I didn't realize how long the adjustment would take. Everyone outside the family treated the twins as celebrities, and that always made me feel guilty. Introducing my newest baby to the twins (now 6) was easier, because they had each other for support.**
>
> *Karen Gromada, Cincinnati, OH*

• Alert visitors to your older child's need for attention. If they don't pick up on this, make a point of calling attention to the value, helpfulness, and uniqueness of the child.

• Let your older child spend the night occasionally with grandparents, relatives, or close friends where he or she can be the center of attention, as long as this is viewed as a treat and not a way to be shut out. Remind the host not to talk too much about the twins while your child is around.

• Be aware that this is a problem that won't go away as the twins get older. Twins will always create interest that a singleton can't compete with. Don't forget to praise and reinforce positive behavior from a child who is trying to deal with this situation.

• Some mothers of twins advise against dressing the twins identically. If you don't call attention to the fact that they're twins, they will get less special attention, and the other child will have fewer reasons to feel jealous and competitive.

Turn To for Twin Tips

Twin Services
PO Box 10066
Berkeley, CA 94709
415-644-0861
This group provides twin-specific information and
services plus a free telephone TWINLINE: 415-644-0861

Twins Magazine
P.O. Box 12045
Overland Park, KS 66212
913-722-1090
This is a bimonthly magazine for parents of multiples.

If Your Baby is Ill or Premature

• If you have advance warning of a problem, explain to the child that sometimes babies are not "perfect" at birth and need special care or longer stays in the hospital. Emphasize the fact that you are doing everything you can to improve the baby's chances by taking care of yourself with proper rest, nutrition, and exercise. Classes for siblings, often sponsored by hospitals, can also be helpful for explaining special circumstances to young children. Fears of the unknown are the worst, so giving your child honest information is important.

• Your child may feel cheated because the baby he or she has been promised for so long has to stay in the hospital longer than expected. Waiting is hard for small children. Do what you can to help your child practice patience.

• Explain prematurity in simple terms such as, "The baby came too soon; he or she wasn't quite ready to be born yet." Depending on the age and maturity of your older child, you may want to include details about just what the baby's problems are. Be sure to include the child when you share news about setbacks or milestones in the baby's progress.

• Explain the infant's illness after birth in terms your child can understand, comparing it with an illness the child has had, if possible.

• Be aware that the child may also be worried about your health and the possibility that you will die. Be honest and reassuring about this too.

• Be sure your child understands that an infant's prematurity or illness is no one's fault: not yours, not the baby's, and certainly not the child's. Some children feel that because they didn't want a sibling, they are to blame for a problem. Reassure your child that this isn't so.

• Be frank about the possibility of the baby dying, if it exists, explaining that it's a rare occurrence and again emphasizing that it's no one's fault.

• Encourage your child to send drawings or other presents to the infant in the hospital.

• Include the hospitalized baby in family life at home. Talk about the baby, display pictures, play in the baby's room, have your child sit and read with you while you use a breast pump, mark a calendar with milestones of the baby's progress in the hospital.

• Let the child visit the hospital with you, and, if possible, see the baby. If the child is young, be sure someone is available to be with him or her in the waiting room. If you think the baby's appearance or the special equipment might frighten your child, be sure to prepare him or her for it beforehand.

• If you are also hospitalized longer than expected, make every effort to let your child visit so that he or she can see that you are not deathly ill. If visiting is not possible, regular telephone calls should help relieve your child's fears.

• Try to arrange for your older child to have just one caregiver while you're gone, and keep to his or her normal routine as much as possible. (This is also important if you will be visiting the baby often after you're discharged.)

• Give your older child all the special love and attention possible. He or she may resent your preoccupation with the sick baby. Tell your child you realize how little time you are able to devote to him or her because of the baby, and that feelings of resentment or even hatred for the baby are natural and understandable.

If You Have a Miscarriage or Your Newborn Dies

• Your child may be very upset after such a loss, or may not express much concern over the loss of an infant he or she has never seen. Relief at having Mom home and well and once again devoted to him or her may be the child's strongest feeling.

• Do raise the issue, just to be sure there is no buried confusion (What happened?), anxiety (Will I die too?), or guilt (Did the baby die because I didn't want him or her?).

• Be aware that questions may come later. Be receptive to them and give honest, open answers, geared to the child's age. Don't hesitate to say, "I don't know why it happened," if that's the case. But do be sure that the child knows that it was not his or her fault that the baby died, even if the child had been wishing that the baby would die or go away. Remind children more than once that they are NOT responsible for the death.

•If you're in the hospital with a miscarriage or stillborn, do let your child visit you there. For children under 5, fear of abandonment by the mother is very strong. In fact the greatest fear of a surviving sibling is that of being left alone. Ask if they wish to see their baby brother or sister, if that is an option.

•Do not exclude siblings from the hospital vigil with a baby struggling for survival.

• If the child is old enough, let him or her mourn with you and attend the funeral if he or she wants to. Don't isolate yourself in your grief, however hard it is not to.

• Explain where the stillborn's body is, or a child will fantasize incorrectly to its whereabouts. If there is a grave, offer to take the child there.

• Be sure your child knows it's all right to talk about the baby and to mention him or her by name. You may want to give your child a memento to remember the baby by. Let your child know that grief is a normal emotion that does not pass quickly. Don't hesitate to seek professional help for yourself or your child if you think it's necessary.

> **Our infant son died of crib death when our first son was 2. We were all in shock, and to our surprise, our 2-year-old cried with everyone else. We told him the baby had stopped living as we do and is now with God, and we will someday see him again. Now, at 4 1/2, he still has sad moments for his baby brother. Then we think of the fun times we did share with him. And we end it with a smile.**
> *Kim Bricker, Park Ridge, NJ*

• Be tolerant of behavior changes in your child, such as clinging and whining, aggressiveness, bed-wetting and nightmares, and realize they are temporary responses to stress. Give your child all the love and attention you can.

• Help your child realize that those unintentionally hurtful comments he or she overhears, such as, "It's for the best," "You can have other children," or "At least you didn't get to know the baby" are not meant to be unkind. They're made by people who don't understand and don't know what to say.

You're Not Alone and Don't be Alone:

Support groups and resources are an absolute must at times like this. Call, or encourage anyone you know dealing with such a sadness to use any of the following resources.

The Pregnancy and Loss Center is a national clearinghouse that networks with other groups, offers a quarterly newsletter and has books available through a mail order catalog.

The Pregnancy and Infant Loss Center
1421 E. Wayzata Blvd.
Wayzatà, MN 55391
612-473-9372

Compassionate Friends, Inc., is a nationwide organization offering support to bereaved parents who have experienced the death of a child. For addresses of local chapters, enclose a self-addressed stamped envelope and write to:

Compassionate Friends
P.O. Box 3696
Oak Brook, IL 60522-3696
708-990-0010

The National Sudden Infant Death Syndrome Foundation will send information on dealing with a loss from crib death. For more information send a self-addressed stamped envelope to:

National SIDS Foundation
10500 Little Patuxent Parkway, Ste. 420
Columbia, MD 21044
1-800-221-SIDS

Call the national number for either of these peer support groups in your area: AMEND (314)487-7582 or SHARE (618)234-2415.

INDEX

PRACTICAL BOOKS FOR TODAY'S PARENTS

This bestselling babyfood and toddler cookbook has over 200 child-tested recipes plus practical feeding advice for new parents.

FEED ME I'M YOURS   **$6.95**

Over 1000 of the best "it worked for me" parenting ideas from diapering to childproofing to getting kids ready for preschool.

PRACTICAL PARENTING FOR THE FIRST FIVE YEARS   **$6.95**

Fabulous cookbook to help wean children on to better-for-you snacks and meals. Brown bag ideas, microwave quickies, milk-free cooking plus good tips for shopping.

THE TAMING OF THE CANDY MONSTER
$7.95

Everything your sitter needs to know! From vital phone numbers on the opening page to a medical release form; play & bedtime tips, first aid info & more.

DEAR BABYSITTER HANDBOOK
$3.95

MaMa & PaPa Bear share their exciting news--there's going to be a new baby bear! Unisex KoKo Bear goes through pregnancy, birth, homecoming--and a bit of jealousy.

THE NEW BABY AT KOKO BEAR'S HOUSE $3.95

I'M THE BIG BROTHER
in blue cotton:
S(2-4) M(4-6) L(6-8)
$12.00

I'M THE BIG SISTER
in pink cotton:
S(2-4) M(4-6) L(6-8)
$12.00

Add new ideas to your repetoire of "I Love Yous," from using sign language to foreign language to other new and easy-to-use ideas.

101 WAYS TO TELL YOUR CHILD 'I LOVE YOU' $5.95

The best tips and ideas for kids' parties for years 1-8. Games, food, decorations,themes, age-related considerations, etc. Planning & memory record sheets.

BIRTHDAY PARTIES: Best Tips & Ideas $6.95

SPECIAL "Diaper Buster" OFFER *$9.99*
(2 books and adapter, regularly $12.40)

TAKE-ALONG FOLD-UP
POTTY SEAT ADAPTER
This wonderful plastic adapter folds to a 5"
square to fit in your purse (alone, $4.50).

KOKO BEAR'S NEW POTTY
KoKo learns how nice dry diapers can be by
learning to use first a potty seat and then the
toilet. KoKo is still loved even when an accident
happens. KoKo's big bear pants and successes
will delight you and your child (alone, $3.95).

TOILET TRAINING
Helpful advice explaining readiness plus practical
hints for daytime and nightime training. Product
information and resources (alone, $3.95).

OTHER TITLES BY VICKI LANSKY:

_____	TRAVELING WITH YOUR BABY	$2.95
_____	GETTING YOUR BABY TO SLEEP (audio tape)	$9.95
_____	FAT-PROOFING YOUR CHILDREN	$4.95
_____	KIDS COOKING (cookbook for 8-12 yr olds)	$4.95
_____	KOKO BEAR'S NEW BABYSITTER	$3.95
_____	KOKO BEAR'S BIG EARACHE (ear tube surgery preparation) ..	$4.95
_____	SING ALONG AS YOU RIDE ALONG (music book & tape)	$5.95
_____	SING ALONG BIRTHDAY FUN (music book & tape)	$5.95
_____	COMPLETE PREGNANCY AND BABY BOOK (hdbd)	$14.95
_____	DIVORCE BOOK FOR PARENTS: Helping Children Cope	$13.95
_____	PRACTICAL PARENTING FOR THE SCHOOL-AGE YEARS	$5.95
_____	THE BEST OF THE PRACTICAL PARENTING™ NEWSLETTER	$5.95

(last title free with merchandise orders over $10)

practical parenting™

18326 Minnetonka Boulevard, Deephaven, MN 55391, customer service 612-475-3527

TO ORDER, CALL TOLL FREE 1-800-255-3379 (24 HOURS)

TO SEND MERCHANDISE TO ANOTHER ADDRESS:

Name _____

Address _____

City/St _____ Zip_____

daytime phone(_____)_____

To: _____

Address _____

City/St _____ Zip _____

Enclose card from:_____

Enclose check payable to PRACTICAL PARENTING
or

CHARGE TO MY ACCOUNT : _____ VISA _____ Mastercard Exp. Date _____

Account #_____Signature _____

billing address, if different _____

Description of item	quantity	price	total
Free with Merchandise orders over $10:			
Best of Practical Parenting Newsletter Book	1	n/c	

SHIPPING AND HANDLING:	Total for Merchandise
If your order totals	In MN residents add 6% tax of above
up to $5.00 .... add $1.50	Shipping/handling (see chart)
from $5.01 to $10.00 .... add $2.25	
from $10.01 to $20.00 .... add $3.00	Additional $2 for UPS
from $20.01up .... add $4.00	**TOTAL AMOUNT** In U.S. Funds
Optional: add additional $2 for UPS delivery	